zen-on score

PROKOFIEV

ALEXANDER NEVSKY
Cantata for Mezzo-Soprano Solo,
Mixed Chorus and Orchestra, Op.78

Commentary by Minoru Morita

ex-VAAP AGENTS

●Boosey & Hawkes Music Publishers Ltd.
for the United Kingdom and British Commonwealth (except Canada)
and Republic of Ireland
●Les Editions du Chant du Monde, Paris
pour la France, la Belgique, le Luxembourg,
l'Andorre et les Pays francophones de l'Afrique
●Musikverlag Hans Sikorski, Hamburg
für Deutschland, Dänemark, Griechenland, Island, Israel,
Niederlande, Norwegen, Portugal, Schweden,
Schweiz, Spanien und Türkei
●Edition Fazer, Helsinki for Finland
●BMG Ricordi S. p. A., Milano per Italia
●G. Schirmer, Inc., New York
for The United States of America, Canada and Mexico
●Universal Edition A.G., Wien, für Österreich
●Zen-On Music Co.,Ltd., Tokyo, for Japan

zen-on music

第4曲「立て、ロシアの民よ」自筆スコア第1頁
4: "Arise, People of Russia!" (Autograph page 1).

「立て、ロシアの民よ」自筆スコア第2頁
"Arise, People of Russia!" (Autograph page 2).

プロコフィエフ（左）とエーイゼンシテイン（右）
Sergei Prokofiev (left) and Sergei Eisenstein (right).

映画『アレクサーンドル・ネーフスキイ』制作中に撮影されたユーモラスな写真
プロコフィエフ（右）、エーイゼンシテイン（中央）
Sergei Prokofiev (right) and Sergei Eisenstein (center), a shot while
making the *Alexander Nevsky* film.

プロコフィエフ
カンタータ《アレクサーンドル・ネーフスキイ》
作品78

解説　森田稔

プロコーフィエフ (1892-1953) は革命直後の1918年にロシアを去り、アメリカからヨーロッパへと転じて、西欧でピアニスト・作曲家として活躍していた。しかし、ソ連とのつながりも捨てたわけではなく、ソ連に残っている友人との文通は続いていたし、実際に1927年には、ソ連へ3カ月にわたる大規模な演奏旅行を行っている。この時に彼はソ連のパスポートも得ていて、彼のソ連国籍が確認されている。その後、彼は1929年と'32年に1回、'33年と'34年にはそれぞれ2回、そして'35年に1回と、繰り返しソ連を訪れ、さまざまな仕事をしていた。そのような経過をへた後、彼は1936年になって、やっとパリの自宅を引き払い、家族全員（妻リーナと二人の息子）を連れて、完全にモスクワの人となったのであった。

その間に、映画音楽では『キージェ中尉』(1933) の仕事が大きな成果を上げていた。とくに、そこから編曲し直した組曲(1934)は、国の内外で大きな評判をとっていた。彼はこうして完全にソ連に復帰したが、西欧との関係は続いていた。'36年11月から'37年2月に掛けてのヨーロッパ・アメリカ旅行、そして翌'38年1月から4月に掛けての、やはりヨーロッパ・アメリカへの旅行が続いている。とくに後者は、結局彼の最後の外国旅行ともなったが、実り多い旅行でもあった。この時彼は、ハリウッドの映画製作現場に親しく立ち会い、大いに刺激を受けた。彼はハリウッドからモスクワの親友ミャスコーフスキイへ出した手紙（1938.3.2.付け）で、滞在予定を少し延ばすことを告げながら、その理由を3つ挙げている。そのうち2つは、予定になかった演奏会が入ったことであるが、3つ目の理由として「ハリウッドが私に対して示した予期せぬ興味」を指摘している。さらに言葉を継いで、「君はこの点について少し文句を言っているようだが、でもこの領域はとても現代的で、その周辺に多くの多様な可能性と限りない興味を伴っている」と述べて、映画音楽に対する大きな関心を露わにしている。

プロコーフィエフ夫妻は実際にハリウッドのディレクターに招待されて、大スターたちとも直接顔を合わせたり、近代的な撮影の現場を目の当たりにし、仕事にも誘われて、大いに興奮したが、彼らはモスクワに居を据えたばかりであったし、子供たちをモスクワに置いていたから、今ハリウッドに留まることは不可能であった。その代わり、彼がモスクワに帰って間もなく、モンタージュ理論で世界の映画界で注目を浴びていた、そしてまた

ハリウッドでも仕事をした経験のある、ソ連が誇る大監督エーイゼンシテイン(1898-1948)から、協力を求められたのである。彼は一も二もなく仕事を引き受けた。これは彼にとって映画に係わる三度目の経験であった。

彼の二作目の映画音楽『スペードの女王』は1936年に作曲されたが、映画そのものが完成されなかったので、彼の音楽は使用されなかった。この年には、メイエイルホーリドの『ボリース・ゴドゥノーフ』への劇付随音楽や、タイーロフの『エヴゲーニイ・オネーギン』への音楽を書いたが、いずれも本体が中止に追い込まれて、ここでも彼の音楽が実際に鳴り響くことはなかった。いずれも1936年、プーシキンの没後百年を記念する年の出来事であった。この年こそ、ショスタコーヴィチが最初の批判を受けた年であり、芸術領域でのスターリン主義の介入があからさまになった時期であった。プロコーフィエフにしてみれば、映画音楽や劇音楽だけでなく、その前に書いたバレエ音楽『ロメオとジュリエット』もまた、上演までの苦難の道を続けている時期であった。

それに較べて、エーイゼンシテインとの仕事は順調そのものであった。エーイゼンシテインもまた、形式主義批判にさらされていて、かなり撮影が進んでいた前作の『ベージン草原』(1937年)が、完成を目前にしながら、放棄せざるを得ない状況に追い込まれていた。映画『アレクサーンドル・ネーフスキイ』は、監督にとっても、作曲家にとっても文字どおり起死回生のチャンスを与えてくれることになった。第2次世界大戦前夜、ナチス・ドイツが台頭し、その脅威がソ連にもひしひしと迫っているときに、13世紀にドイツ騎士団の侵略を打ち破って祖国を守った、ロシア史の英雄“アレクサーンドル・ネーフスキイ”は、まさに時宜にかなった恰好の題材であった。

プロコーフィエフがアメリカから帰ってきて間もなく、1938年5月にエーイゼンシテインから正式な協力依頼が来た。エーイゼンシテインは20年代後半には西欧にしばしば旅行していて、プロコーフィエフもすでにパリで会って、互いに顔は知り合っていたが一緒に仕事をするのは、これが初めてであった。エーイゼンシテインの方がプロコーフィエフよりも6歳ほど若かったが、彼らはともに雑階級出身の天才であり、そして、革命前後の激動の時代に、それぞれの芸術分野でロシアの最前衛の芸術運動に育まれ、国際的にも広く注目されていたという意味で、共通点も多かった。もっともこの国際的なつながり故に、スターリン主義の時代には当局の疑いを受けやすく、また実際に苦難の道を強いられた点でも、彼らは似ている。その上、エーイゼンシテインはユダヤ人であったから、苦難はいっそう大きかったといえよう。そのような社会的状況のなかで、二人とも政府の文化政策上の要請に応えて、大衆にも分かり易い、‘社会主義リアリズム’の名で呼ばれるソ連的な様式を目指して、模索していた。

彼らは二人ともに、高度な職業主義に培われた、厳しい芸術家であった。プロコーフィエフは『アレクサーンドル・ネーフスキイ』の作曲過程について、映画完成直後に、ある文集へ一文を寄稿して、具体的な仕事ぶりについて報告している。それによると、彼はエーイゼンシテインが「非常に繊細な音楽家でもあった」ので、「仕事への興味が増した」とか、「われわれは3つのマイクを使い、そ

れら３つの流れを混合（"ミキシング"）するのに高度な技術が必要であったが、録音レバーを握っていたヴォーリスキイはこの点では、比類がなかった」などと述べて、自分の音楽的な仕事が、監督を始め録音技師にも深く理解されたことに、大きな喜びを表明している。ついでながら、"ミキシング"という言葉が強調されていて、当時この語が新語であったことが分かる。

実際、エーイゼンシテインはオペラ演出でも高名なメイエルホーリドの直接の弟子であり、音楽については専門的な素養があった。また、ヴォーリスキイ (1903-) も録音技師ではあったが、彼のプロコーフィエフに関する回想を読むと、彼がキエフ音楽院の出身で、ホロヴィッツやニコラーエフ（ショスタコーヴィチの先生）の師として名高いブハーリスキイに師事した、本格的なピアニストでもあったことが分かる。ヴォーリスキイはプロコーフィエフの仕事ぶりについて、次のような証言を残している。

エーイゼンシテインはプロコーフィエフに『氷上の激戦』を作曲するように言って、すでに撮影されていたその場面のラッシュを見せながら、彼がロシアの騎士たちとドイツの騎士たちの戦闘をどのように編集するかを詳しく述べ、作曲家にカトリックの古い聖歌を使った音楽で、全体の長さが「４分半から５分」の曲を依頼した。これに対して、作曲家は聖歌は20世紀風には響かないと言ってその使用を断り、「今日の聴衆が聞き慣れたスタイルで作曲しなくてはならないが、彼らがそれを遠い昔の音楽だと、つまり、画面と結びついたときに、彼らが観客としてそれを13世紀の時代の音楽だと思うように、彼らを"巧

みに騙す"必要がある」と主張したという。また、「スコアは互いに対立するロシアとドイツの２部分に分けるべきで、その際、ドイツの部分は"ロシア人の耳には不快なもの"であるべきだ」と述べ、「いくつかの楽器をマイクの前で実験して、音がひどく不快なものになるように、そして何の楽器の音か分からないように、楽器の性格を歪めることが必要だ」と主張したという。「結局、実験の結果、プロコーフィエフはホルンを選び、それをマイクの至近距離に置いて、とくに歪みを付けて録音した。――合唱と管弦楽のためのカンタータでは、プロコーフィエフはこのパートをイングリッシュ・ホルンとトロンボーンに変えた―― 効果は抜群だった…。」その後プロコーフィエフはスコアを完成し、自ら"Peregrinus"を歌いながらピアノで演奏して、作業用の材料として円盤に録音したとヴォーリスキイは書いているので、今後アーカイヴの整理が進めば、作曲家の自作自演のこの録音が発見されて、聴くことができるようになるかも知れない。

ヴォーリスキイはさらに、プロコーフィエフがマイクの配置の仕方に工夫を凝らしたことを書いている。マイクを別々にして、楽器とマイクとの距離を近づけたり離したりすることによって、'巨大なオーボエ'の音や、'小さなトランペット'の音が得られることを確認するなど、彼はありとあらゆる可能性を検討して、録音用に特別な編曲を行ったという。そして当時同時使用が可能であった４本のマイクを縦横に使い分けた。ヴォーリスキイは「指摘して置かねばならないと思うことに、『アレクサーンドル・ネーフスキイ』の映画録音用のスコアは、後の管弦楽用のスコア

とは大きく異なっているということがある。これら二つのスコアの検討は極めて興味深い、独自なテーマである」と述べている。「全オーケストラができるだけ隔離された4つのマイクロフォン［3つではない―森田］に分けて配置され……、プロコーフィエフ自身は指揮をせずに、録音機の音をチェックした。オーケストラの音のミキシング用のメモとして、彼は私のために、当時われわれが名付けた、特別の"カンニング・ペーパー"を書いてくれた。この"カンニング・ペーパー"はオーケストラのグループの間で、あちらを際立たせたり、こちらを際立たせたりして、グループ間の関係を決めるのにとても役立った」という。なお、このことに関してはプロコーフィエフ自身も書き残していて、こちらは日本語にも訳されているので直接読むことができる（園部四郎他訳『プロコフィエフ・自伝・評論』音楽之友社、昭和39年、pp.168-170）。

エーイゼンシテインとプロコーフィエフの仕事は快調に進み、映画は予定よりも5カ月も早く、1938年11月に完成した。12月1日の映画の封切りは大成功で、スターリンの絶大な賞賛を得て、エーイゼンシテインと主役のチェルカーソフはレーニン勲章を与えられ、プロコーフィエフの音楽も賛辞を浴びた。プロコーフィエフにとって、これはソ連で達成した最大ヒットであり、映画はソ連各地で大入りを続けた。プロコーフィエフはすぐに映画音楽からの管弦楽曲を構想したが、すでに述べたように、映画音楽は独自の方法を取り入れていたので、演奏会用の作品に組み替えるためには、管弦楽法も曲の構成も根本的な作り替えが必要になった。しかしその仕事も

順調に進み、1939年5月17日には、ガガーリナのメゾ・ソプラノ独唱、作曲者自身の指揮するモスクワ・フィルハーモニー管弦楽団と合唱団によって、演奏会用のカンタータ《アレクサーンドル・ネーフスキイ》は初演され、これまた大成功を収めた。しかし同時に、この時期を境として、スターリンの大粛清は大詰めに入り、第2次世界大戦への緊張が高まって、プロコーフィエフの西欧との絆は完全に切れてしまうのである。

楽曲解説

アレクサーンドル・ネーフスキイ (1220?-63) はロシア史上に実在する英雄である。アレクサーンドルはノーヴゴロド公から、後にヴラディーミル大公となった。彼は1240年ノーヴゴロド公のときに、ネヴァー川の戦いでスウェーデン軍を大破したことから、"ネーフスキイ（ネヴァー川の）"のあだ名で呼ばれる。引き続き1242年には、ドイツ騎士団の襲撃を、凍結したチュード湖上で撃破して勇名を馳せた。ロシアがキプチャク・ハーン国の支配を受けた、いわゆる「タタールのくびき」の時代にあって、ロシアの栄光を守った英雄として、中世ロシアでもっとも尊敬されている人物である。ピョートル大帝が首都ペテルブルグに、この英雄の名を冠した修道院を建設したことでも知られる。

曲は7つの楽章からなる。激しく対立するロシアとドイツが、際だった音楽的性格の違いによって描き上げられ、これが曲の構成の基本になっている。ハ短調（苦悩するロシア）、変ロ長調とニ長調（明るいロシア）、嬰ハ短調（ドイツの侵略者）などと、各調の性格を巧みに生かした調性配置が注目される。3部

形式をとる楽章が多いが、第5楽章や第7楽章のように、自由な形式による絵画的な描写音楽も特徴的である。

1. モンゴル圧制下のルーシ

モルト・アンダンテ、ハ短調、4分の3拍子。

全楽章のなかでもいちばん短く、全曲への序奏の役割を果たしている。モンゴルの支配を受けていたこの時代の、厳しい悲劇的な雰囲気を描き上げている。エーイゼンシテインの台本には、この音楽が伴われる映画の冒頭の情景について、「モンゴルの攻撃で荒野と化したロシアの悲しい戦（いくさ）の跡。人骨と鎧帷子、錆び付いた槍の堆積。雑草に覆われた原野、燃え朽ちた材木の廃墟」と記されているとい

う。冒頭、二重付点の装飾音型を伴う長2度の旋律はロシアの英雄叙事詩の世界を想起させる。[譜例1]

オーボエ、バス・クラリネット、ファゴットなど木管楽器が受け渡し合う旋律は、ロシア民謡的色彩の濃い性格で、これが4オクターヴもの広い音域を隔てたプロコーフィエフ独自の楽器法によって、荒廃したロシアの大地を、悲痛な思いを込めて描いている。

2. アレクサーンドル・ネーフスキイの歌

レント、変ロ長調、4分の2拍子。

一転して、明るい変ロ長調の主和音の響きが、ソプラノを除いた合唱のつややかな色彩によって強調される。[譜例2]

変ロ長調は終曲（第7曲）の調子でもあり、

【譜例1】

【譜例2】

【譜例3】

このカンタータ全体の主調と考えることができる。変ロ長調は、オペラ『戦争と平和』の大詰めでロシアの勝利を讃える合唱など、愛国的な場面で頻繁に使われているし、『交響曲第5番』や『ピアノ・ソナタ第7番』など、後期のプロコーフィエフが、一貫して祖国ロシアを賛美する、象徴的な意味を感じていた調子である。ルゴフスコーイの詩もまた、ドイツ騎士団の襲撃を受ける2年前に、アレクサーンドル・ネーフスキイの軍隊がネヴァー川でスウェーデン軍の侵略を撃退した、ロシアの愛国的な記憶を讃えている。中間部のピユ・モッソの部分で、ロシアの吟遊詩人バヤンの楽器グースリを思わせる、弦のピチカートとアルベジオの響きに乗せて、ロシア軍の戦闘ぶりが描かれる。

って侵略されたプスコーフの町の悲劇的な状況を暗示する。そこにアンダンテにテンポを変えて、ソプラノを除いた合唱が、ロシア人にはなじみのない言葉と旋律で、カトリック教徒の不気味な祈りの歌をうたう。ふたたび不協和な金管の全奏が帰ってきて、続く中間部では弦楽器群が、第6音の高いイ短調のドリア旋法で、異邦人の支配に苦しむロシア人の泣き歌を歌う。しかしここにも、ホルンを中心とした金管の奏する、侵略軍の冷酷な軍靴の刻むリズムのような、角張った支配者のテーマが聞こえている。[譜例3]

そして冒頭の金管の不協和な強奏が再現され、これがつなぎのようになって、ふたたびアンダンテに帰り、カトリック教徒の不気味な祈りが、やや短縮されて繰り返される。

3. プスコーフに駐留する十字軍

ラルゴ、嬰ハ短調、4分の4拍子。

嬰ハ短調の主和音にトロンボーンの長7度音（嬰ロ音）が無遠慮に加わる、金管楽器の強奏する不気味な不協和音が、ドイツ軍によ

4. 立て、ロシアの民よ

アレグロ・リゾルート、ハ短調、2分の2拍子。

鐘やタムタムの警鐘に応えて、祖国の防衛に立ち上がろうと呼びかける、ロシアの勇士

【譜例4】

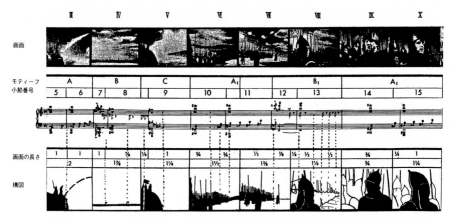

【'氷上の激戦'のシークエンスにおける視聴覚モンタージュ実例のコンティニュイティ】(山田和夫氏の御好意により転載)
このシーンのフィルムのカット割りと心理的描写に見事に音楽付けがなされている事がわかる。

たちの力強い雄叫びである。中間部は明るいニ長調に転じて、「祖国ルーシに、偉大なルーシに、敵を入れてはならない」と、叙情的なロシア民謡的な節まわしによって、いっそうロシア的な世界が強調される。[譜例4]

5. 氷上の激戦

この楽章はカンタータの中心で、もっとも長い楽章である。しかし内容的には、ドイツ騎士団とロシア軍との氷上での激戦を、戦闘が目前に展開されるかのように描写的に描いていて、伝統的な楽曲形式で説明できるような音楽形式は取っていない。映画の画面展開をそのまま彷彿させるという意味で、もっとも映画的な楽章とも言えよう。

曲は霧深いチュード湖の朝を描く序奏から始まる。映画の台本には「アレクサーンドルは"烏岩"の上に立ち、これから戦闘の行われる原野を眺めている。あたりはまだ夜明けの霧に包まれている。夜が明けてくる。4月の太陽は煙った光をゆっくりと差し込んで、雲の多い夜の空を探り出す」とある。しかしこの静けさのなかにも、すでに不吉な予感は満ちている。序奏の最後で、その予感の全貌が姿を現し(弱音器付きトロンボーン)、それが第3楽章で描かれていたドイツ騎士団[譜例3]の影であることが分かる。ここでの嬰ハ短調はドイツ騎士団の世界である。やがてその全貌が姿を現し、カトリックの祈りの歌が響きわたる。戦闘はドイツ軍の有利に展

【譜例5】

開し、ドイツ軍は「十字軍の戦士は勝利する」と叫びながら、突進する。ロシア軍がこれを迎え打つ。ここでスコモローヒの軍楽がひょうきんな感じで挿入され、応戦するロシア軍を支援する。[譜例5]

ドイツ軍は絶対的に優勢である。しかし、やがて調子は一転してニ長調になり、アレクサーンドルに先導されてロシア軍の勇姿が大きく立ち現れる。[譜例6]

この伸びやかな旋律がニ長調と変ロ長調を行き来して、さっそうとしたロシア軍の戦いぶりを見事に描いている。ドイツ騎士団の雄叫びは、優勢なときには完全5度や完全4度の音程で示されていたが、それがだんだんと崩れて、いまや三全音や増6度などにデフォルメされて、敗色が顕わになる。さらにアダージョの緩やかな動きのなかで、2オクターヴにわたって音階的に駆け昇ったり下りたり

【譜例6】

【譜例7】

する音型によって、融けて崩れてゆく氷が暗示され、ドイツ騎士団の軍勢は湖のなかへと消えていく。ホ短調とハ短調とを行き来する金管の旋律と和声の色彩が、彼らの宿命的な運命を暗示している。[譜例7]

「血みどろの死体が浮かぶ湖面に、霧にかすむ新月の三日月が登り、遠くは薄い水色の煙に包まれている」。そして最後に変ニ長調で、ロシアの賛歌[譜例4]が静かに響く。

6. 死の野原

アダージョ、ハ短調、4分の4拍子。

映画の台本には、「チュード湖畔の夜。辺りに死体が散乱している。不気味な静寂のなか、かすかなうめき声も聞こえる…。高く低く点滅する明かりを持って、女性たちが湖畔をさまよっている。孤独な女性の歌が聞こえる。これはオーリガである。彼女は自分の婚約者を探している」とある。メゾ・ソプラノ独唱による挽歌である。低い7度音を伴う自然短音階の旋律は、典型的なロシア民謡の節回しである。中間部で少し動きを早めて、第3楽章で開かれたドリア旋法の泣き歌の旋律

が出る。激しい戦闘場面を描き上げた第5楽章の緊張を、そっと和らげてくれるような、印象的な緩徐楽章である。

7. アレクサーンドルのプスコーフ入場

モデラート、変ロ長調、4分の4拍子。

合唱に明るいソプラノの音色が加わって、冒頭から祝典的な雰囲気を盛り上げる。曲はアレグロ・マ・ノン・トロッポに転じたあと、調もイ長調になって、合唱が「楽しめ、歌え」と戦勝気分を歌う。ここはメノ・モッソで、中世ロシアの芸人スコモローヒが登場する。これは第5楽章の中頃で、ドイツ騎士団の突撃を迎え打つロシア軍の士気を奮い立たせた芸人集団の再登場である。ここで彼らは軍楽の担当者ではなく、お祭りの立役者に役割が変わっている。そして最後に、ロシアの勝利を讃える歌が、まず男声合唱の変ホ長調で、女声合唱も加わってその増5度上のロ長調、最後に半音下がって変ロ長調に落ちついて、管弦楽のトゥッティとともに、堂々と全曲を閉じる。

解説本文、ロシア語テキストの日本語訳中の人名、地名等は、著者の表記に従いました。

【歌詞対訳】 ───────────森田 稔 訳

слова Владимира Луговского 作詞：ウラディミール・ルゴフスコーイと
и Сергея Прокофьева セルゲイ・プロコーフィエフ

2. Песня об Александре Невском.

2. アレクサーンドル・ネーフスキイの歌

А и было дело на Неве-реке. ネヴァー川のうえでの出来事だった。
На Неве-реке, на большой воде. ネヴァー川のうえ、広大な水のうえ。
Там рубили мы злое воинство. そこで我らは敵の軍勢を打ち破った。
Злое воинство, войско шведское. 敵の軍勢、スウェーデンの部隊を。
Ух! Как бились мы, как рубились мы! ああ！ 我らは戦い、我らは切り合った！
Ух! Рубили корабли по досточкам. ああ！ 舟をこなごなに打ち壊した。
Нашу кровь - руду не жалели мы 我らは自らの血を惜しまなかった、
за великую землю русскую. Гей! 偉大なロシアの大地のために。ヘイ！
Где прошел топор, была улица. 斧が行くところには、道路ができた。
Где летело копье - переулочек. 槍が飛ぶところには、小路ができた。
Положили мы шведов-немчинов, 我らはスウェーデンの異人たちを倒した、
как ковыль-траву на сухой земле. 乾いた大地に、はがねや草のように。
Не уступим мы землю русскую. 我らはロシアの大地を捨てない。
Кто придет на Русь, будет насмерть бит. ルーシに攻め入るものは討たれて死ぬ。
Поднялася Русь супротив врага, ルーシは敵に向かって立ち上がった、
поднимись на бой, славный Новгород! 栄えあるノーヴゴロドよ、戦さへと立て！

3. Крестоносцы во Пскове.

3. プスコーフに駐留する十字軍

Peregrinus, expectavi, 異邦人である私は、期待していた、
pedes meos, in cymbalis. 私の足が、鐘を履いていると。

4. Вставайте, люди Русские.

4. 立て、ロシアの民よ

Вставайте, люди Русские, 立て、ロシアの民よ、
　　на славный бой, на смертный бой, 聖なる戦さへ、決死の戦さへ、
вставайте, люди вольные, 立て、自由の民よ、
　　за нашу землю честную. 我らの汚れない大地のために。
Жмвым бойцам - почет и честь, 生き残った戦士には尊敬と名誉を、
　　а мертвым - слава вечная. そして死んだ戦士には永遠の栄光を。
За отчий дом, за русский край вставайте, 父の家のため、ロシアの国のため、
　　люди русские. ロシアの民よ立ち上がれ。

16

Вставайте, люди Русские,
　　на славный бой, на смертный бой,
вставайте, люди вольные,
　　за нашу землю честную.
На Руси родной,
　　на Руси большой не бывать врагу.
Поднимайся, встань, мать родная Русь!
На Руси родной,
　　на Руси большой не бывать врагу.
Поднимайся, встань, мать родная Русь!
Вставайте, люди русские,
　　на славный бой, на смертный бой.
вставайте, люди вольные,
　　за нашу землю честную.
Врагам на Русь не хаживать,
　　полков на Русь не важивать,
путей на Русь не видывать,
　　полей Руси не танцывать.
Вставайте, люди Русские,
　　на славный бой, на смертный бой,
вставайте, люди вольные,
　　за нашу землю честную!

ロシアの民よ、聖なる戦さへ、
　決死の戦さへ立ち上がれ。
我らの神聖な国土のため、
　自由の民よ立ち上がれ。
祖国ルーシに、
偉大なルーシに、敵を入れてはならない。
母なる祖国ルーシよ、目覚めよ、立てよ！
祖国ルーシに、
偉大なルーシに、敵を入れてはならない。
母なる祖国ルーシよ、目覚めよ、立てよ！
ロシアの民よ、聖なる戦さへ、
　決死の戦さへ立ち上がれ。
我らの神聖な国土のため、
　自由の民よ、立ち上がれ。
敵にルーシを歩かせるな、
　部隊を展開させるな、
ルーシへの道を見せるな、
ルーシの野を歩かせるな。
ロシアの民よ、聖なる戦さへ、
　決死の戦さへ立ち上がれ、
我らの神聖な国土のため、
　自由の民よ、立ち上がれ。

5. Ледовое побоище.

Peregrinus, expectavi,
　pedes meos, in cymbalis,
peregrinus, expectavi.
Vincant arma crucifera! Hostis pereat!
Vincant arma crucifera! Hostis pereat!
Peregrinus, expectavi,
　pedes meos, in cymbalis,
expectavi, expectavi, est.

5. 氷上の激戦

異邦人である私は、期待していた、
　私の足が、鐘を履いていると、
異邦人である私は、期待していた。
十字軍の戦士は勝利する！ 敵は負ける！
十字軍の戦士は勝利する！ 敵は負ける！
異邦人である私は、期待していた、
　私の足が、鐘を履いていると、
　私は期待していた。

6. Мертвое поле.

Я пойду по полю белому,

6. 死の野原

私は白い野原を行く、

полечу по полю смертному.

Поищу я славных соколов,

женихов моих, добрых молодцев.

Кто лежит, мечами порубленный,

кто лежит, стрелою пораненный.

Напоили они кровью алою,

землю честную, землю русскую.

Кто погиб за Русь смертью доброю,

поцелую того в очи мертвые,

а тому молодцу, что остался жить,

буду верной женой, милой ладою.

Не возьму в мужья красивого:

красота земная кончается.

А пойду я за храброго.

Отзавитеся, ясны соколы!

死の野原を飛んでいく。

私は栄誉ある鷹を探す、

私の婿を、勇敢な若者を。

剣に打たれて横たわるもの、

矢に傷ついて横たわるもの。

彼らは赤い血を流す、

栄光の大地、ロシアの大地に。

ルーシのために善良な死を捧げたもの、

私は彼の死んだ眼に口づけする、

そしてまだ命の残っているものには、

私は忠実な妻、愛しい恋人となる。

私は美しい男を夫にはしない、

地上の美しさには終わりがあるから。

私は勇敢なものに従う、

勇敢な鷹よ、応えておくれ！

7. Въезд Александра во Псков.

На великий бой выходила Русь.

Ворога победила Русь.

На родной земле не бывать врагу.

Кто придет, будет на смерть бит.

Веселися, пой, мать родная Русь!

На родной Руси не бывать врагу.

Не видать врагу наших русских сел.

Кто придет на Русь, будет на смерть бит.

Не видать врагу наших русских сел.

Кто придет на Русь, будет на смерть бит.

На Руси родной, на Руси большой не бывать врагу.

На Руси родной, на Руси большой не бывать врагу.

Веселися, пой, мать родная Русь!

На Руси родной, на Руси большой не бывать врагу.

Веселися, пой, мать родная Русь!

На великий праздник собралася Русь.

Веселися Русь! Веселися Русь, родная мать!

7. アレクサーンドルのプスコーフ入場

ルーシは偉大な戦さへ出立した。

ルーシは敵に勝利した。

祖国の大地には、敵を入れてはならない。

攻め入るものは、死をもって打たれる。

楽しめ、歌え、母なる祖国ルーシよ！

祖国ルーシには、敵を入れてはならない。

我らのロシアの村々に、敵を見ることはない。

ルーシに攻め入るものは、死をもって打たれる。

我らのロシアの村々に、敵を見ることはない。

ルーシに攻め入るものは、死をもって打たれる。

祖国ルーシに、偉大なルーシに、敵を入れてはならない。

祖国ルーシに、偉大なルーシに、敵を入れてはならない。

楽しめ、歌え、母なる祖国ルーシよ！

祖国ルーシに、偉大なルーシに、敵を許さない。

楽しめ、歌え、母なる祖国ルーシよ！

偉大な祝日に、ルーシが集合した。

楽しめルーシ！ 楽しめルーシ、生みの母よ！

Sergei Prokofiev

"Alexander Nevsky," Cantata, Opus 78

Commentary by Minoru Morita

Sergei Prokofiev (1892-1953) left Russia in 1918, immediately after the Revolution, for the United States, and then moved to Western Europe, where he was active as a pianist and composer. However, he did not necessarily isolated himself from the Soviet Union; he remained in touch with his friends remaining in the Soviet Union, where he actually visited in 1927 on a three month long concert tour. On that occasion, he expressly identified himself as a Soviet citizen by acquiring a Soviet passport. He revisited the Soviet Union many times, once each in 1929 and 1932 and twice each in 1933 and 1934, for various artistic activities. After those swings between his fatherland and the West, in 1936 he finally cleared away his residence in Paris, and took all his family (wife Lina and two sons) with him to become a full-time citizen of Moscow.

In the meantime, he had been very successful in film music with his "Lieutenant Kijé" (1933). Especially, the suite version (1934) he adapted from the screen music was highly acclaimed both in the Soviet Union and elsewhere. When he permanently returned to the Soviet Union, Prokofiev kept his ties with Western Europe unbroken. From November 1936 to February 1937, he toured Europe and America, and from January to April 1938,

he again visited both Europe and America. Especially the latter, which eventually was his final trip abroad, proved very fruitful. During the travel, he personally inspected a filmmaking scene in Hollywood, and was keenly stimulated. In a letter from Hollywood to his good friend Nikolay Myaskovsky (dated March 2, 1938), Prokofiev told him of his plan to extend the trip a little, and cited three reasons for the change in schedule. Two of them were previously unscheduled concerts, but the third was "unexpected interest Hollywood showed to me" as he pointed out. By adding, "You seem to be complaining a little about this point, but this field is very contemporary, accompanied by many possibilities and objects of immense interest around it," Prokofiev did not conceal his great interest in cinema music.

Sergei and Lina Prokofiev were actually invited by a Hollywood director to an occasion to meet big stars in person, and directly witnessed scenes of modern cinematography. He was much excited by an offer of an opportunity to work, but it was impossible for the Prokofievs to stay in Hollywood then as they had just settled down in Moscow and their children were waiting there for the parents. Instead, soon after his return to Moscow, Prokofiev was asked by Eisenstein to work with him.

Sergei Eisenstein (1898-1948), a great film director the Soviet Union was proud of, had attracted the note of the world filmdom with his 'montage' theory and had also experienced work in Hollywood. Prokofiev had no reason to hesitate. This was his third experience in film music.

His second work for cinema, *The Queen of Spades*, composed in 1936, was never used because the film itself was not completed. In the same year, he wrote incidental music for *Boris Godunov*, a theatrical play by Vsevolod Meierkhol'd, and music for *Eugene Onegin* by Alexander Tayrov, but again these compositions never actually sounded because the theatrical projects themselves ended up abortive. Both were events in 1936, the 100th anniversary of Pushkin's death. It exactly was the year in which Shostakovich suffered the first official criticism, the period in which Stalinists began their undisguised intervention in artistic affairs. For Prokofiev, film music and theatrical music were not the only fields in which he experienced difficulties, but the ballet music *Romeo and Juliet*, composed earlier, also had a hard way to go before it was finally staged.

In contrast, his work with Eisenstein was well before the wind. Eisenstein, too, had been criticized for his alleged formalism, and was obliged to give up his previous project *Bezhin Meadow* (1937), which was about to be completed. The film *Alexander Nevsky* was to give both the director and the composer the last chance for survival. It was on the eve of World War II, and the Soviet Union was exposed to the menace of the emerging Nazi Germany with growing imminence. Alexander Nevsky, a great hero in the Russian history who in the 13th century defended his country by defeating the invading German Knighthood, was indeed a timely theme to choose.

Soon after Prokofiev returned from the United States, in May 1938, he received a formal request for cooperation from Eisenstein. The director had often visited Western Europe in the latter half of the 1920s, and the composer had met him in Paris. So they were no strangers to each other, but its was the first occasion for them to work together. Eisenstein was six years younger than Prokofiev. They had many attributes in common: both were geniuses from "the miscellaneous class," having grown up in the most avant-garde artistic movements in Russia in their respective fields and attracting extensive international interest. Precisely for their international connections, though, they invited the suspicion of the official authorities during the Stalinist days, and actually had to experience hardships, another common factor in their lives. Moreover, things must have been harder on Eisenstein because of his Jewish blood. In this social context, both were groping for a way to comply with the requirements of the cultural policy of the government, a Soviet style which would be easy for the masses to understand, the so-called "Socialist realism."

Both were stern artists trained in the traditions of strict professionalism. Immediately after the completion of the film, Prokofiev contributed to a collection of writings a report on the specifics of his process of composing the music for *Alexander Nevsky*. According to his report, his "interest in the work was enhanced" by the personality of Eisenstein who "was a very delicate musician," and "we used three microphones, and 'mixing' the three streams of sounds from them required sophisticated skills, in which respect Vol'sky, holding the recording levers, had no parallel." In these words, the composer expressed his joy at the profound understanding of his musical work by the director and the audio engineer. Incidentally, he emphatically used the term "mixing," suggesting that it was a new word at the time.

In fact, Eisenstein was a direct pupil of Meierkhol'd, who was also highly reputed as an opera director, and therefore no amateur in music. Boris Vol'sky (1903-), the audio engineer for this film, also was a professionally trained pianist who, according to his own memoir of Prokofiev, graduated from the Kiev Conservatory of Music and studied with Vladimir Pukhal'sky, well known as a teacher of Vladimir Horowitz and Leonid Nikolayev (who in turn taught Shostakovich). Vol'sky left the following testimony in his memoir regarding the way Prokofiev worked.

Eisenstein told Prokofiev to write music for "The Battle on the Ice" and showed him the rushes of the scene which had already been shot. The director explained in detail how he would edit the shots of the battle between Russian and German knights, and asked the composer to write a piece of music of "4-$\frac{1}{2}$ to 5 minutes" in total length, using an old Catholic chant. The composer rejected the idea, saying that a chant would not sound like 20th century music, and reportedly maintained, "I have to compose in a style familiar to the audience of today, but they have to be 'tactfully cheated' into believing that it was an ancient piece of music, in other words, when tied with the visual scenes, the music should be taken by the audience as a work of the 13th century." Prokofiev is also reported to have said, "The score should be divided into two opposing sections for Russia and Germany, and the German section should sound 'unpleasant to the Russian ear'," and "it is necessary to experiment with a number of instruments before the microphone and distort the characters of the instruments so that they sound very disagreeable and cannot be identified by the sounds they make." "Eventually, as a result of this experiment, Prokofiev chose French horns, which were positioned extremely close to the microphone and whose sounds were recorded with deliberate distortions —— in the cantata for chorus and orchestra, Prokofiev replaced the instruments for this part with an English horn and trombones —— the result was splendid....." Later, when he finished the score, Prokofiev sung "Peregrinus" with his own accompaniment on the piano to get it recorded on a disc as a working aid, according to Vol'sky. Future progress of the work to organize the relevant archives may unearth this recording by the composer himself, and we may have an opportunity to hear it.

Vol'sky also tells us what ingenuity Prokofiev showed in working out unusual microphone arrangements. By using separate microphones for different instruments or bringing a microphone extremely close to or far away from the instrument, he made sure that the sounds of a 'huge oboe' or of a 'tiny trumpet' could be produced. The composer tested all the possibilities he could think of, and made a special adaptation for recording, the engineer recollects. And he positioned four microphones, the maximum number that could be used simultaneously in those days, in all conceivable arrangements. Vol'sky continues, "What I find noteworthy is that the score of *Alexander Nevsky* for cinematographic recording greatly differed from the later orchestral score. These two scores present us with an extremely interesting, unique theme to study." "The whole orchestra was divided into groups each matching one of four microphones [not 'three' —— Morita] positioned as far apart from one another as practicable ...... and he wrote for me special 'cribs', as we called them then, to give me hints on mixing the sounds of the orchestra. These 'cribs' proved very useful in determining the relationships among the groups of the orchestra, which required highlighting of one group sometimes and another at other times." Prokofiev himself also touched on this episode (*Prokofiev, Autobiography and Critical Essays*).

Eisenstein and Prokofiev's project made smooth progress, and the film was completed in November 1938, five months ahead of the schedule. When released on December 1, the film proved very successful, winning Stalin's generous admiration. Eisenstein and Nikolay Cherkasov, who played the title role, were decorated with Lenin Orders, and Prokofiev's music also received many praises. Prokofiev immediately planned to adapt the screen music for independent orchestral performance, but the original work for the soundtrack used so unique methods that its remaking into concert music required fundamental changes in orchestration and structure of the music. The project nevertheless was before the wind again, and the concert cantata *Alexander Nevsky* was premiered on May 17, 1939 by the Moscow Philharmonic Orchestra and Choir under the direction of the composer himself with V.D. Gagarina, mezzo soprano, as soloist, which also achieved a great success. At the same time, however, Stalin's wholesale purge entered into its most intense phase and the tension, which would culminate in World War II, heightened to sever Prokofiev's ties with Western Europe once and for all.

"Alexander Nevsky", Cantata

Alexander Nevsky (1220?-63) is a hero whose name actually appears in the history of Russia. Alexander was the Duke of Novgorod, and later became the Archduke of Vladimir. In 1240, as the Duke of Novgorod, he overwhelmed Swedish troops in the Battle of the Neva River, and this victory earned him the nickname of Nevsky (the adjective of the Neva River). Then in 1242, his reputation for bravery was further enhanced when he defeated the assaulting German Knighthood on the frozen Lake Chud. He is one of the most respected of Medieval Russian personalities as a hero who defended the glory of Russia, when the country was in "the Age of the Tartar Yoke" under the rule of Kipchak Khanate. Nevsky is also known for the monastery which Peter the Great built in Petersburg, the then Russian capital, and christened after him.

The cantata consists of seven movements. Russia and Germany, archrivals to each other, are depicted in distinct musical contrast, which constitutes the very basis of the structure of the work. Particularly noteworthy is the allocation of keys making skillful use of the character of each by having C minor representing Russia in agony, B flat and D majors, Russia in joy, and C sharp minor, the German aggressors. Most of the movements are in a ternary form, but the fifth and seventh are free in form, characterized by picturesque ways of musical portrayal.

No. 1: Russia under Mongolian Tyranny

Molto andante, C minor, three-four time.

The shortest of all the movements, this part serves as an introduction to the whole cantata. The stern tragic atmosphere of the days under Mongolian rule is well depicted. Eisenstein's script reportedly describes the beginning scene of his film, which this movement accompanies, as "remains of Russia's sorrowful battles, devastated by Mongolian assaults. Heaps of human bones, armored garments and rusty lances. A wilderness covered with weeds, ruins of burnt out timber." At the beginning, a melody using major seconds with double-dotted ornamental figures reminds the listener of the world of epics of Russian heroes (Ex. 1).

The melody handed over among oboes, a bass clarinet and bassoons from one to another is filled with elements of Russian folk songs, and depicts the devastated Russian land with a bitter sentiment in Prokofiev's unique instrumentation spanning over four octaves.

No. 2: Song of Alexander Nevsky

Lento, B flat major, two-four time.

In sharp contrast to the first movement, the joyful sound of the tonic triad is emphasized by the lustrous color of the chorus with the soprano part absent (Ex. 2).

The B flat major, also the key of the finale (seventh movement), can be considered the main tonality of the whole cantata. It is the key in which Prokofiev in his later years consistently found a symbolic meaning of admiring his fatherland Russia, frequently used in patriotic scenes including the chorus hailing Russia's victory in the final scene of the opera *War and Peace*, as well as in Symphony No. 5 and Piano Sonata No. 7. The verse by Vladimir Lugovskoy also admires Russians' patriotic memory of the defeat of invading Swedish troops by Alexander Nevsky's army on the Neva River, two years before the assault by the German Knighthood. In the intermediate *più mosso* part, the fight by the Russian troops is portrayed over the pizzicati and arpeggi of the strings, which the listener might associate with the instrument called *gusli*, the favorite instrument of Russian troubadours known as *bayans*.

No. 3: The Crusade in Pskov

Largo, C sharp minor, four-four time.

A major seventh (B sharp) by trombones intrudes on the tonic triad of the C sharp minor. Weird discords played forte by the brass suggests the tragic situation of the

[Ex. 1]

[Ex. 2]

[Ex. 3]

Town of Pskov conquered by the German army. The tempo then changes to *andante*, and the chorus without soprano sings a weird song of the Catholic prayer in a language and melody unfamiliar to Russians. Discords by the brass *tutti* return and, in the following intermediate part, the strings sing a moaning song of the Russians suffering under the rule of aliens in the Dorian mode of A minor having a higher sixth tone. Here again, however, the rigid theme of the conquerors, played by the brass with horns in the fore, is heard, suggesting the cruel rhythm of the aggressors' combat boots (Ex. 3).

The forceful discords by the brass at the beginning are resumed, and they serve as a bridge back to *andante*, in which the weird Catholic prayer is repeated somewhat reduced in length.

No. 4: "Arise, People of Russia!"

Allegro resoluto, C minor, two-two time.

Brave Russian warriors' forceful call on fellow countrymen to arise in the defense of the fatherland is sung in response to the alarming sounds of the campana and the tam-tam. The key shifts to the joyous D major in the intermediate part, where the Russian world is further emphasized by the verse, "Never let the enemy set foot in our land Russia, the great Russia," sung in a lyric Russian folk song-like melody (Ex. 4).

No. 5: The Battle on the Ice

This is the longest movement constituting the core of the cantata. In content, it portrays the fierce battle on the ice between the German Knighthood and the Russian army as if it was fought before the listener's eyes, but has no musical form which can be associated with any traditional formality. It may be the most cinematographic movement in the sense that it directly suggests visual developments in the film.

The movement begins with an introduction depicting a foggy morning on Lake Chud. The cinema script says: "Standing on the 'crow rock', Alexander is looking over the field where a battle is about to begin. The scene is still wrapped in the morning mist. Day begins to dawn. The April sun slowly radiates smoky rays, and searches the foggy night sky." However, this tranquil is already full of ill omens. At the end of the introduction, the ill omens fully reveal themselves (muted trombones), and they are found to be the shadow of the German Knighthood

portrayed in the third movement (Ex. 3). The C minor used here represents the world of the German Knighthood. Its full shape is uncovered in the meantime, and the Catholic prayer song reverberates. The battle develops in favor of the Germans, who make a dash, shouting "Crusaders win!" The Russians meet the enemy. Here is inserted a military music piece of *skomorokhi* (buffoons) in a funny way to support the Russians fighting back (Ex. 5).

The Germans are at an absolute advantage. Yet the key suddenly changes to D major, and the Russian troops led by Alexander make an imposing appearance (Ex. 6).

This vivacious melody moves back and forth between D and B flat majors to splendidly depict the gallant fight by the Russian soldiers. The war cries of the German Knighthood, expressed in perfect

【Ex. 4】

【Ex. 5】

【Ex. 6】

【Ex. 7】

fifths or fourths when they were dominant, have gradually decayed, and are now deformed into tritones or augmented sixths to suggest their emerging signs of defeat. Further in slow *adagio* moves, figures running up and down over two octaves suggest melting and collapsing ice; the German troops disappear into the lake. The colors of the melody and chords by the brass moving back and forth between E and C minors imply their fatality (Ex. 7).

"On the surface of the lake where bloodstained corpses are floating, a fog-blurred new moon rises, and the landscape in the distance is wrapped in a pale blue smoke." At the end, the hymn to Russia (Ex. 4) calmly sounds in D flat major.

No. 6: The Field of the Dead

Adagio, C minor, four-four time.

The cinema script says: "By Lake Chud at night. Corpses lie all around. Through the weird tranquil, faint groans are heard..... Carrying lamps of intermittently fluctuating brightness, women are wandering on the lakeside. A solitary woman's song is heard. Oliga is singing. She is looking for her fiancé." It is an elegy by mezzo soprano. The melody on a natural minor scale accompanied with a low seventh is typical of Russian folk songs. In the intermediate part, the melody of the moaning song in the Dorian mode, which was heard in the third movement, returns at a slightly faster tempo. This is a memorable slow movement, which gently eases the tension of the fifth movement depicting the fierce battle.

No. 7: Alexander Enters Pskov

Moderato, B flat major, four-four time.

The chorus is joined by the bright tone color of the soprano part, enhancing a festive atmosphere from the very beginning. After accelerating to *allegro ma non troppo*, the key also shifts to A major, and the chorus hails the victory, "Have fun, sing!" Here appear medieval Russian buffoons known as *skomorokhi*. They are the group of entertainers who, in the middle of the fifth movement, enhanced the morale of the Russian soldiers meeting the dash of the German Knighthood. Their role is now one of star players in the festival instead of a military band. And finally, a hymn to the Russian victory is sung first by the male voices of the choir in B flat major, then joined by the female voices in B major, up by an augmented fifth, and at the end settling down in B flat major, a semi-tone below, to close the whole cantata magnificently.

Sergei Prokofiev: *Alexander Nevsky*, Cantata, Opus 78
Verse
By Vladimir Lugovskoy and Sergei Prokofiev
(Retranslated from Japanese translation by Minoru Morita)

No. 2: Song of Alexander Nevsky

It happened on the Neva River. / On the Neva River, on the vast stretch of water. / There we defeated the enemy troops. / The enemy troops, the Swedish units. / Oh, we fought, and we and they slashed one another! / Oh, we chopped their boats into pieces. / We spared no blood of our own, / In defense of the great Russian land. Hey! / Where the ax went, there was opened a road. / Where the lance flew, there was made an alley. / We beat the alien Swedes, / Like feather grass on a dry ground. / We shall never give up the Russian land. / Whoever invades Russia will be attacked and die. / Russia has arisen against the enemy. / Glorious Novgorod, arise to fight!

No. 3: The Crusade in Pskov

As a foreigner, I expected, / My feet to be shod in cymbals.

No. 4: "Arise, People of Russia!"

Arise, people of Russia, for the holy battle, for the deadly battle! / Arise, free people, to defend our chaste land! / To the living warriors, respect and honor are due, and to the dead, eternal glory. / To defend the home of our fathers, the land of Russia, arise people of Russia! / Arise, people of Russia, for the holy battle, for the deadly battle! / Arise, free people, to defend our sacred territory! / In our fatherland Russia, in our great Russia, no enemy should exist. /

Our mother Russia, wake up and stand! / Russia, in our great Russia, no enemy should exist. / Our mother Russia, wake up and stand! / Arise, people of Russia, for the holy battle, for the deadly battle! / Arise, free people, to defend our sacred territory! / Never let the enemy set foot in Russia, never let them deploy their forces. / Never show them paths to Russia, never let them tread the fields of Russia. / Arise, people of Russia, for the holy battle, for the deadly battle! / Arise, free people, to defend our sacred territory!

No. 5: The Battle on the Ice

As a foreigner, I expected, / My feet to be shod in cymbals. / As a foreigner, I expected, / The warriors of the Crusade to win, the enemy to lose! / The warriors of the Crusade to win, the enemy to lose! / As a foreigner, I expected, / My feet to be shod in cymbals. / As a foreigner, I expected.

No. 6: The Field of the Dead

I go over the white field. / I fly over the field of the dead. / I look for the glorious falcon, / My bridegroom, the brave young man. / Some lie hacked with swords, / Others lie shot with arrows, / They shed red blood, / On the glorious soil, the Russian land. / One who died a good death for Russia, / I will kiss his dead eyes, / And of one who is still alive, / I will be the faithful wife, the loving sweetheart. / I will not marry a handsome man, / Because earthly beauty has its end. / I will follow the brave, / Brave falcon, respond to my call!

No. 7: Alexander Enters Pskov

Russia marched out to the great battle. / Russia defeated the enemy. / The land of our country should let in no enemy. / Those who invade will be rewarded with death. / Have fun, sing, our mother Russia! / Our Russia should let in no enemy. / Our Russian villages shall ever see no enemy in. / Those who invade will be rewarded with death. / Our Russia, the great Russia, should let in no enemy. / Our Russia, the great Russia, should let in no enemy. / Have fun, sing, our mother Russia! / Our Russia shall forgive no enemy. / Have fun, sing, our mother Russia! / On the great festive day, Russia has gathered. / Have fun Russia, have fun, Russia, mother of ours.

English translation by Hiromichi Matsui

❧ ❧ ❧

　このスコアでは、すべての楽器がハ調、つまり実音の通りに書かれている。しかしながらパート譜では、バス・クラリネット、テナー・サキソフォーンおよびトランペットは変ロ調で、クラリネットは変ロとイ調、　イングリッシュホルン（コーラングレ）とホルンはヘ調で書かれなければならない。

　スコア上ではトランペット、ホルン、ティンパニ、グロッケンシュピール（オーケストラ・ベル）とシロフォンは調号で表記しているが、それらのパート譜では各音符に臨時記号を付けて書くべきであろう。

　金管楽器のファンファーレのパートは弱音器を用いるが、それ以外のパートは弱音器を用いない。いくつかのファンファーレはオフ・ステージで少し距離を置いて演奏される（スコアに *in distanza* と書かれる）。演奏者はスコアに *loco* と表示されているところで定位置に戻る。

　打楽器は次のようなグループに分けられるべきである。

> 1. トライアングルとマラカス
> 2. タンブリン
> 3. スネア・ドラム（小太鼓）
> 4. バス・ドラム（大太鼓）
> 5. シンバルとウッド・ブロック

タムタムは第1パート（第3,4,5楽章）と第2パート（第7楽章）に書き分けられている。よって楽器は第1奏者と第2奏者の間に置かれるべきである。鐘（*Campana*）は第3奏者（練習番号27以前）と第4奏者（27以降）に振り分けられる。よってその楽器は彼ら演奏者の間に置かれるべきである。

　ティンパニ、シロフォン（木琴）とグロッケン（オーケストラ・ベル）はそれぞれの奏者が受け持つ。鐘（*Campana*）の音は低くあるべきであるが、タムタムに消されてはならない。

　マラカスはジャズで使われるキューバの楽器で、乾燥した種子が詰まった2つの大きな木ノ実から出来ている。ウッドブロック（*legno*）の音はカスタネットに似ている。

　ハープは2人の奏者によるのがよいであろう。

　バス・クラリネットが持たない低いCの音（第1楽章の最後のソロ）は、ダブル・バスーンが演奏すべきだろう。

　　──ソヴィエト国立出版所ムージカからの"プロコフィエフ作品集成16A"（1965年）の注記による

❧ ❧ ❧

❧ ❧ ❧

In this orchestral score, all the instruments are noted in C, namely as they sound. In the separate parts, however, the bass clarinet, the tenor saxophone and the trumpets should be written in B flat, the clarinets in B flat and A, and the English horn and the French horns in F.

Although key signatures are used for the trumpets, French horns, timpani, glockenspiel (orchestra bells) and xylophone in the score, an accidental should be appended to each applicable note in the parts.

The brass should be muted for the fanfare part, but not for any other part. Some fanfares should be played off stage at some distance (noted *in distanza* in the score). The players should return to their regular positions where *loco* is written in the score.

The percussion should be divided into the following groups:
1. Triangle and maracas
2. Tambourine
3. Snare drum
4. Bass drum
5. Cymbals and wood-block

Different parts are specified for the tam-tam between the 3rd, 4th and 5th movements (the first part) and the 7th movement (the second part). Therefore the instrument should be placed between the first and second players. The tubular bells (campana) are also shared between the third (before 27) and fourth (after 27) players. Here again, the instrument should be located between them.

The timpani, xylophone and glockenspiel (orchestra bells) should be played by their respectively designated performers. The sounds of the campana should not be very loud, but not be drowned by the tam-tam.

The maracas, originally from Cuba and often used in jazz, consists of two large nuts filled with dried seeds. The wood-block (*legno*) sounds like castanets.

Two harps should preferebly be used, played by two performers.

The low C note the bass clarinet cannot cover (in its final solo in the first movement) should be taken over by the double bassoon.

——Note to the *Collected works of Prokofiev 16a* (1965) published by the Soviet State Music Publishers *Muzyka*.

❧ ❧ ❧

● 楽 器 編 成 ●

ORCHESTRA

1 Flauto piccolo	1 Piccolo Flute	ピッコロ
2 Flauti	2 Flutes	フルート 2
2 Oboi	2 Oboes	オーボエ 2
1 Corno inglese	1 English Horn	イングリッシュ・ホルン (=コーラングレ)
2 Clarinetti (in Si♭/La)	2 Clarinets (in B♭/A)	クラリネット (変ロ/イ) 2
1 Clarinetto basso (in Si♭)	1 Bass Clarinet (in B♭)	バスクラリネット (変ロ)
1 Saxorfono (in Si♭)	1 Tenor Saxophone (in B♭)	テナー・サキソフォーン
2 Fagotti	2 Bassoons	ファゴット (=バスーン) 2
1 Contrafagotto	1 Double Bassoon	コントラファゴット (=ダブルバスーン)
3 Trombe (in Si♭)	3 Trumpets (in B♭)	トランペット (変ロ) 3
4 Corni (in Fa)	4 Horns (in F)	ホルン (ヘ) 4
3 Tromboni	3 Trombones	トロンボーン 3
1 Tuba	1 Tuba	テューバ
Timpani	Timpani	ティンパニ
Triangolo	Triangle	トライアングル
Legno	Wood Block	ウッドブロック
Tamburino	Tambourine	タンブリン
Tamburo	Snare Drum	スネア ドラム (小太鼓)
Maracas	Maracas	マラカス
Piatti	Cymbals	シンバル
Gran cassa	Bass Drum	バス ドラム (大太鼓)
Tam-tam	Tam-Tam	タムタム
Campana	Chimes	鐘
Campanelli	Orchestra Bells (Glockenspiel)	オーケストラ・ベル (グロッケンシュピール)
Silofono	Xylophone	シロフォン (木琴)
Arpa	Harp	ハープ
Violini Ⅰ	Violins Ⅰ	第1ヴァイオリン
Violini Ⅱ	Violins Ⅱ	第2ヴァイオリン
Viole	Violas	ヴィオラ
Violoncelli	Violoncellos	チェロ
Contrabassi	Double Basses	コントラバス

ALEXANDER NEVSKY
Cantata for Mezzo-Soprano solo,
Mixed Chorus and Orchestra
1. Russia under Mongolian Tyranny

Sergei Prokofiev, Op.78

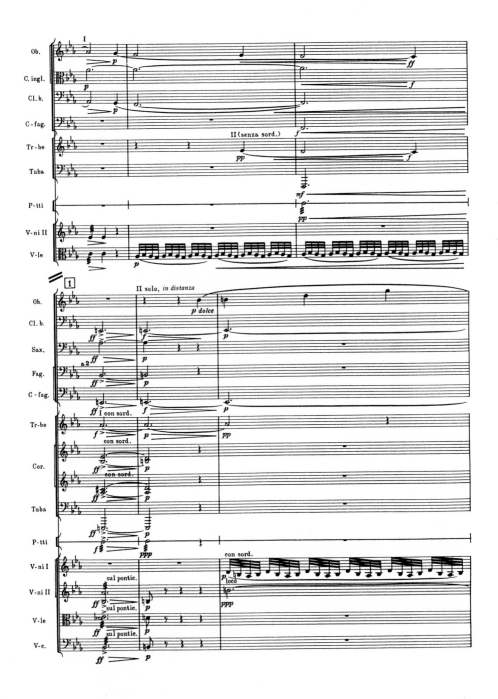

II. Song of Alexander Nevsky

43

44

46

III. The Crusade in Pskov

50

60

64

IV. "Arise, People of Russia!"

66

70

Русь!

На Ру - си род - ной, на Ру - си боль - шой не бы - вать вра - гу.

74

Под - ни - май - ся, встань, мать род - на - я Русь!

ков на Русь не ва - жи - вать, пу - тей на Русь не ви - ды-вать, по -

V. The Battle on the Ice

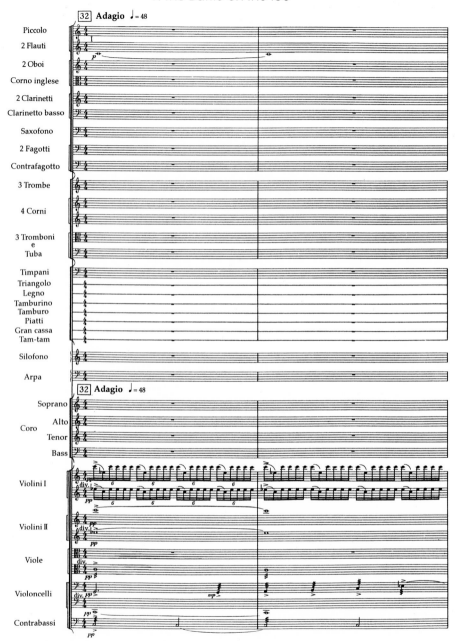

82

89

90

104

107

114

126

130

56
Picc.
Fl.
Ob.
C. ingl.
Cl.
Cl. b.
Sax.
Fag.
C-fag.
Tr-be
Cor.
Tr-ni
e
Tuba
56
Archi
pizz.
div.
div.
pizz.
pizz.
div.
div.
pizz.
div.
unis.
arco
unis.
arco
unis.
pizz.
pizz.

143

148

150

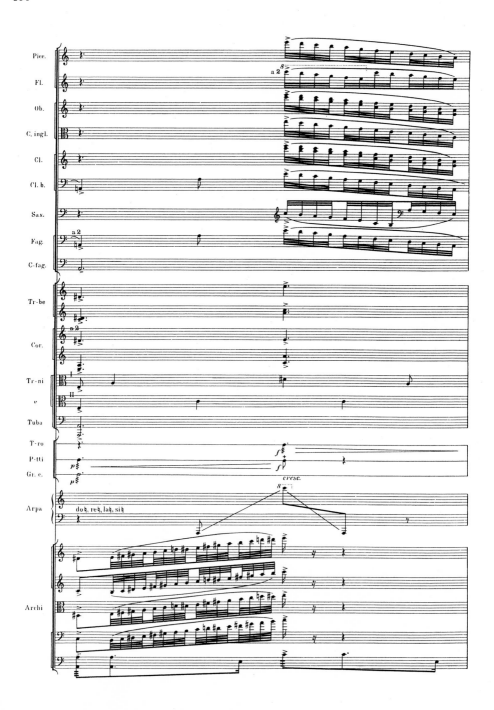

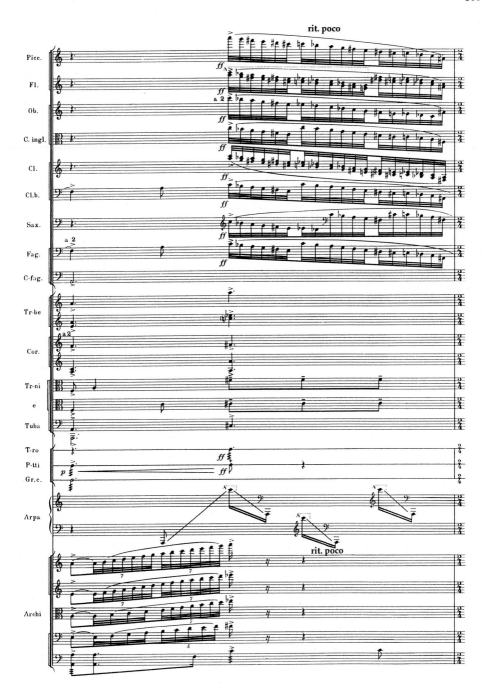

VI. The Field of the Dead

VII. Alexander Enters Pskov

176

184

190

プロコフィエフ

カンタータ《アレクサーンドル・ネーフスキイ》 ●

解説・ロシア語訳 ——————————— 森田 稔

英訳 ——————————— 松居弘道

第1版第1刷発行 ——————————— 1999年6月20日

第1版第6刷発行 ——————————— 2010年1月20日

発行 ——————————— 株式会社全音楽譜出版社

——————————— 東京都新宿区上落合2丁目13番3号〒161-0034

——————————— TEL・営業部03・3227-6270

——————————— 出版部03・3227-62 0

——————————— URL http://www.zen-on.co.jp/

——————————— ISBN978-4-11-892669-8

1001069

ZEN-ON POCKET SCORES